History of the World

Greek Mythology

Don Nardo

KIDHAVEN PRESS

THOMSON

GALE

Detroit • New York • San Diego • San Francisco
Boston • New Haven, Conn. • Waterville, Maine
London • Munich

On cover: Apollo and the crow, 490 B.C.

Library of Congress Cataloging-in-Publication Data

Nardo, Don, 1947–
  Greek Mythology / by Don Nardo.
    p. cm. — (History of the world)
  Includes bibliographical references.
  Summary: Includes the origins of the gods and humans—The adventures of the mighty Heracles—Heroes of the Trojan War—Three timeless tales of love.
  ISBN 0-7377-1035-7
  1. Mythology, Greek—Juvenile literature. [1. Mythology, Greek.] I. Title. II. Series.
  BL783 .N37 2002
  398.2'0938—dc21

2001007833

Contents

Chapter One
  The Origins of the Gods and Humans   4

Chapter Two
  The Adventures of the Mighty Heracles   14

Chapter Three
  Heroes of the Trojan War   24

Chapter Four
  Three Timeless Tales of Love   34

For Further Exploration   43

Index   45

Picture Credits   47

About the Author   48

The Origins of the Gods and Humans

L ike people in all times and places, the ancient Greeks told and retold stories about the creation of the world, the gods, and human beings. The Greeks believed that many gods existed. Each god controlled some aspect of nature or a region of the earth or sky. The Greek gods looked and acted very much like humans. The gods got married, had children, fought among themselves, and sometimes made mistakes. One important factor separated them from people, however. That was their tremendous power. The gods could alter nature or destroy humans and their cities at will. So people had no choice but to recognize and respect the power wielded by the gods.

Chaos and the Early Gods
The Greek myths about the creation of the gods and humans explain how that huge difference in power

came about. The first of these stories begins uncounted ages ago, when there was only a great hollow void. That void was called Chaos. Inside it, the seeds of all things swirled together in a shapeless mass. After a very long time, Chaos gave birth to two children. One was Nyx, or Night. The other was Erebus, or Darkness.

More time passed. Then suddenly, in some mysterious way, from the blackness of Nyx and Erebus sprang Eros, or Love. Eros made it possible for things to come together and grow. He brought light to pierce the darkness. And through his influence, order began to appear in the void. The heavier elements slowly settled and became the earth, while the lighter

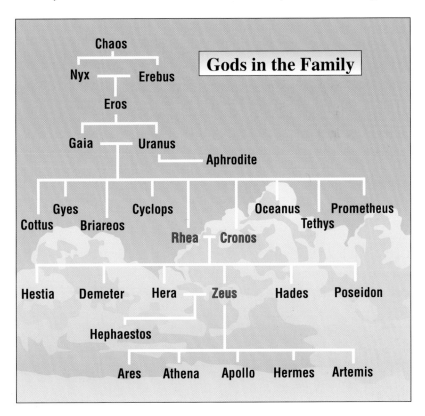

Gods in the Family

parts drifted upward and became the sky. Two deities emerged to control these regions. One was Gaia, or Mother Earth; the other was Uranus, or Father Sky. Far below the earth, a dark, scary region called Tartarus remained.

Gaia and Uranus had many children. The first members of the brood were huge and misshapen, and they possessed the power of earthquakes and volcanoes. Three of them were monsters, each having fifty heads and a hundred hands. Their names were Cottus, Gyes, and Briareos. Next came huge creatures that had

One of the cyclopes forces some men to serve him.

a single eye in the middle of their foreheads. These were known as the cyclopes.

Finally, Gaia and Uranus produced the twelve Titans. These gods looked similar to humans but were much larger and stronger. Among them were Oceanus and Tethys, who took charge of the sea; Rhea, a mother goddess; and Cronos, the youngest and most powerful of all.

Wars in Heaven

Like nearly all mothers, Gaia loved all of her children, no matter how ugly. But Uranus hated his children, especially the monsters and cyclopes. So he banished them to Tartarus. This distressed Gaia greatly. She, Cronos, and the other Titans rebelled against Uranus. During the fight, Cronos stabbed his father, and drops of Uranus's blood showered down. The wounded Uranus finally lost the battle. And Cronos imprisoned him in the shadowy regions of Tartarus.

Now that Uranus was out of the way, mighty Cronos assumed the kingship of heaven. He married his fellow Titan Rhea, and they began to have children of their own. But Cronos feared that his offspring might rebel against him just as he had rebelled against Uranus. So as soon as each child was born, Cronos swallowed it whole. This happened five times. Poor Rhea wanted to stop her husband from eating their children. When she gave birth to her sixth child, Zeus, she hid the baby in a cave. She knew that Cronos would expect her to hand over a child for him to devour. So she tricked him by handing him a giant stone wrapped in baby's clothes. Like a fool, he grabbed and swallowed the stone.

By saving her son Zeus, Rhea set in motion a series of events that led to another war in heaven. When Zeus grew to manhood, he learned about the horrible fate of his brothers and sisters. With the help of his grand-mother, Gaia, the young god secretly fed Cronos a dose of very strong medicine. This made the king of the Titans vomit up all those he had swallowed. Out popped Cronos's and Rhea's first five children: Hestia, Demeter, Hera, Hades, and Poseidon.

Zeus and his five sisters and brothers joined forces and waged war on Cronos and most of the other Titans. As they joined in battle, the sea heaved in

Aboard his magnificent chariot, Zeus prepares to hurl one of his deadly thunderbolts.

great waves and the earth shook. The shaking was so violent, in fact, that it could be felt in dark Tartarus.

The Olympians

At last, Zeus and his forces won the battle. They cast Cronos and most of the other Titans down into Tartarus. Zeus and his companions then divided up the earth among themselves. They lived in a magnificent palace high atop Mt. Olympus, the tallest mountain in Greece. So they came to be called the Olympians.

Zeus controlled the Olympians and took his sister Hera as his wife. She became the guardian of marriage and childbirth. Meanwhile, Zeus's brothers acquired their own, though lesser, realms. Poseidon took control of the sea, for example. And Hades became ruler of the Underworld, including dark Tartarus. Zeus's sisters had their own important roles. Hestia became protector of the hearth, and Demeter oversaw agriculture. The goddess of love, Aphrodite, was not Zeus's sister. She had been born in the sea where some blood had fallen when Cronos had attacked Uranus.

Most of the other powerful Olympians were Zeus's children. These included Ares, god of war; stately Athena, goddess of wisdom and war and the protector of civilized life; the handsome Apollo, lord of prophecy, truth, and the healing arts; the swift and cunning Hermes, the messenger god; Apollo's twin sister Artemis, goddess of the moon and the hunt;

An ancient carving depicts the goddess Artemis (in the center) surrounded by the other Olympians.

and Hera's son, the kind and peace-loving Hephaestos, god of fire and forges.

The First Humans

In this bygone era when the gods acquired their great power, there were still no humans on earth. The most popular story about the creation of humans involved the Titan Prometheus. He had helped Zeus in the great war in heaven. So Zeus had not exiled him to Tartarus. Zeus gave him the task of making races of mortal animals and humans, and Prometheus fashioned some people from mud. To set them apart from the animals, Prometheus gave them the physical form of the divine gods. But this was clearly not enough. He saw that these mortals had to struggle hard to find food and build shelters. He wanted to give them fire to make their lives easier. But Zeus forbade it, saying the humans were not worthy of the divine spark of fire.

Luckily for humanity, the bold Prometheus decided to defy Zeus. The Titan snatched a bit of fire from the sun and brought it down to earth. There, he taught the humans how to cook their food. He also taught them to create weapons, tools, houses, ships, and many other things.

When Zeus saw that Prometheus had disobeyed him, he was furious. To punish Prometheus, Zeus ordered two giants to seize the Titan. They and Hephaestos bound Prometheus to a rock on the summit of a faraway mountain. There, each day a gigantic eagle gnawed at Prometheus's liver. At night, when the bird was gone, the liver grew back. And the next day the chained god had to endure the same agonies again.

Zeus also punished the humans. He noticed that all of the humans were male. So he ordered Hephaestos to mold a woman out of clay. Hephaestos did so, and the gods called her Pandora. Zeus told Hermes to take Pandora down to earth. She carried with her a large, sealed jar that Zeus had given her, but she did not know its contents. Eventually, her curiosity got the better of

A French artist's painting of Prometheus bound on the mountaintop.

her and she opened the jar. Out rushed a swirling tor-
rent of evils—disease, hatred, greed, and many others.
Finally, the creation of the gods, humans, and human
society, with all the ills that trouble it to this day, was
complete.

Chapter  Two

The Adventures of the Mighty Heracles

T he ancient Greeks were a very inventive and creative people. They built magnificent temples and crafted beautiful statues of people and animals. They also introduced many of the ideas and institutions familiar today. One of these is democracy, the system of government in which people vote for their leaders. Theaters and sports competitions like the Olympics are other ancient Greek inventions.

Many of these accomplishments occurred in the fifth and fourth centuries B.C., about twenty-three hundred to twenty-five hundred years ago. Modern historians refer to this period as the Classical Age. Yet the Classical Greeks were not the first people to create a high civilization in Greece. And they were well aware of that fact. The ruins of huge, very ancient fortresses dotted their landscape. Moreover, their myths were

Ancient Greece

filled with the exploits of great heroes of the dim past. The stories claimed that these larger-than-life figures had performed wondrous deeds and had actually spoken with the gods. That is why the Classical Greeks called that long-ago legendary time the Age of Heroes.

The Madness of Heracles

The most famous and beloved of these early heroes was Heracles (whom the Romans called Hercules). Heracles' physical strength was unmatched among mortals. Indeed, Heracles was even stronger than some of the gods. He was also a humble man who owned up to his mistakes and willingly accepted his punishments.

Heracles' worst mistake, which led to his most memorable punishment, involved his wife and children. His wife, Megara, was the daughter of Creon, king of the great Greek city of Thebes. Heracles came to love Megara deeply and she bore him eight children, all of whom he loved just as much. Unfortunately, the goddess Hera hated Heracles. Her divine husband, Zeus, had slept with Heracles' mother, and Hera was jealous and wanted revenge. So she made the strongman fall into a fit of madness. Not realizing what he was doing, Heracles killed his wife and six of his children.

When Heracles finally came to his senses and saw what he had done, he was filled with sorrow and guilt. He traveled to Delphi, where Apollo's oracle lived. (The oracle was a priestess who conveyed messages from the god to humans.) The oracle told Heracles to go to Mycenae, in southern Greece, and seek out its king, Eurystheus. Eurystheus would know what to do.

The Twelve Labors

Following the oracle's advice, Heracles made his way to Mycenae. Eurystheus welcomed the strongman and told him that he must perform a number of labors. These tasks were so difficult that an ordinary person would find them nearly impossible. Only after Heracles had completed these labors would he be cleansed of the guilt of his terrible crime.

Heracles readily agreed to perform the labors, which numbered twelve in all. The first was to kill the Nemean Lion, a huge creature that could not be wounded by weapons. Charging at the beast, the strongman grasped the lion around its neck and strangled it. For his second labor, Heracles slew the Hydra, a monster that killed many cattle and terrorized the countryside. The Hydra had a huge body and nine heads. Heracles grabbed the creature and

Mighty Heracles wrestles the Nemean Lion in this seventeenth-century painting.

squeezed it with all his strength. Then he burned the Hydra's heads with a flaming branch to keep them from growing out again. Finally, he cut off the heads and buried them under a heavy rock.

Amazons and Golden Apples

Heracles' other labors were no less difficult. In the third, he tracked down and brought back alive the Cerynitian Hind, a fabulous stag with horns of gold. In the fourth, he captured a large and vicious boar that had destroyed several villages. The fifth labor required Heracles to clean out the stables of a king named Augeas, which were unbelievably filthy because thousands of cattle had lived in them for years. In his sixth labor, Heracles drove away a flock of huge birds that had been killing humans and animals. To complete the seventh task for Eurystheus, Heracles captured a beautiful but savage bull and carried it back to Mycenae. In the eighth labor, the strongman brought back a herd of man-eating horses. For his ninth labor, Heracles delivered to Eurystheus the girdle of Hippolyta, queen of the Amazons, a famous tribe of warrior women. The tenth labor required the hero to travel to the far edge of the earth; there, he captured a herd of cattle belonging to a monster named Geryon, who had three bodies and three heads. And in the eleventh labor, Heracles had to bring back a box of golden apples, a treasure guarded by a fearsome dragon.

The twelfth and last of Heracles' labors was the most difficult and dangerous of all. Eurystheus ordered him to descend into the Underworld. There, he had to capture Cerberus, the monstrous three-headed dog that guarded the realm of the dead. The god Hermes and goddess Athena guided the man down into the Underworld. There, Heracles fought

Heracles battles the nine-headed Hydra to complete his second labor.

and wounded Hades, the lord of that realm. Then the strongman approached Cerberus. Heracles threw his arms around its neck and refused to let go until the dog gave up the struggle. Then the strongman carried Cerberus back up to the earth's surface. King Eurystheus had no intention of keeping the dangerous creature, of course. So Heracles had to lug it back to its place in the Underworld.

Heracles Joins the Gods

Heracles had finally completed all twelve of the seemingly impossible labors. These tasks had taken many years. But the strongman had finally paid the price for the sin of killing his wife and sons.

The twelve labors were not the only heroic deeds Heracles performed, however. He also helped the Olympian gods defeat a race of giants. These menacing creatures had sprung from the blood droplets that fell after the Titan Cronos stabbed his father, Uranus. Zeus feared the giants for good reason. Though the Olympians were incredibly strong, the giants were immune from death at the hands of any god. Therefore, to win the battle, Zeus needed the aid of a mortal hero. So, he called on the tremendously strong and valiant Heracles. Unable to withstand the attack of the world's strongest man and the Olympians combined, the giants went down to defeat.

Eventually, Heracles joined the gods permanently. One day, the strongman was seriously burned by the

An eighteenth-century painting shows Heracles dragging the hideous Cerberus out of the Underworld.

blood of a centaur, a creature that was half man and half horse. Heracles sought the advice of the Delphic oracle once again. Through the oracle, the gods instructed him to erect a funeral pyre, a stack of wood and brush for burning the dead. Heracles should lie down atop the pyre and wait, the oracle said.

Obediently, Heracles had one of his surviving sons build the pyre. When the dying hero laid down on it,

Heracles is shown on his funeral pyre only seconds before rising into the realm of the gods.

his relatives and friends were startled by a huge bolt of lightning that exploded from above. Then they saw a column of smoke rise swiftly into the sky. When they looked back at the pyre, Heracles' body was gone. Their hearts were filled with joy when they realized what had happened. The gods had taken the mighty Heracles into their realm, granting him the gift of eternal life.

Chapter Three

Heroes of the Trojan War

T he ancient Greeks viewed the story of the Trojan War as the most inspiring and important of all their myths. The legendary tale described a long war against the prosperous city of Troy, located in what is now western Turkey. An alliance of Greek kings sailed across the Aegean Sea and sacked and burned Troy. Homer, a legendary eighth-century B.C. Greek, told much of the story in his fifteen-thousand-line poem, the *Iliad*.

Modern scholars uncovered Troy's ruins, showing that it was a real city. But no one knows if the war in the myth actually happened. The important thing is that the ancient Greeks strongly believed such a war occurred. And they held its leading characters in awe, seeing them as great heroes of a glorious bygone age.

The Greeks Lay Siege to Troy
Some of the heroes of the Trojan War were Greek kings and warriors. The others were Trojan warriors.

The Greek kings gathered to attack Troy after a Trojan prince named Paris ran off with a Greek queen named Helen. She was not just any queen. Helen was widely seen as the most beautiful woman in the known world. And she was the wife of Menelaus, the king of the important Greek city of Sparta. The other Greek kings had earlier pledged to protect any man Helen married. So now they came to Menelaus's aid in his effort to win back his wife.

The Greek kings and their armies met at Aulis, in eastern Greece. Agamemnon, the king of Mycenae and Menelaus's brother, led the trip. Some of the other leaders included Achilles, the greatest warrior in Greece; Ajax, a giant of a man whose fighting skill was second only to that of Achilles; and Odysseus, the wily king of the island kingdom of Ithaca.

As the war begins, a fierce battle rages on the plain in front of the walls of Troy.

When the Greeks reached the flat and windy plain of Troy, they were sure they would win the battle. After all, they greatly outnumbered the Trojans. However, Troy was not easily defeated. The Trojans had many heroes of their own. First and foremost among them was Hector, Paris's brother and the son of Troy's king, Priam. Hector was the finest living warrior next to Achilles. Another factor in the Trojans' favor was their city's towering stone walls. None of the Greek attacks could penetrate these great barriers. So the war dragged on for many years.

A Quarrel in the Greek Camp

Eventually, though, in the tenth year of the siege, the Trojans suddenly gained the advantage. Luckily for them, in the Greek camp Achilles and Agamemnon had a terrible quarrel. The angry Achilles retired to his tent and refused to come out and lead the Greeks in battle as he had so often done. Without Achilles, the Greeks were unable to stop the attacking Trojans. Led by Hector, the Trojans drove the Greeks back to their beach encampment. Hector smashed into the Greeks so hard that he struck panic into their hearts. And they ran away like cattle escaping from a savage lion.

It seemed the Greek cause would be lost. Then Achilles, who was still brooding in his tent, received a visit from his closest friend, brave Patroclus. Patroclus begged to borrow and wear Achilles' armor. That way the Trojans might think that Patroclus was Achilles and retreat. Achilles agreed to Patroclus's request, and

The goddess Athena stops Achilles from killing Agamemnon during an argument between the two men.

wearing his friend's armor, Patroclus led the Greeks against the Trojans. Thinking that mighty Achilles himself was attacking them, the fearful Trojans began to fall back. Even Hector retreated for a while. But

The Trojans and Greeks fight for possession of the body of Patroclus.

soon, Hector turned and faced Patroclus. Because he was a much greater fighter, Hector easily slew Patroclus and stripped off Achilles' armor.

Two Great Heroes Fight to the Death

Hearing of his friend's death, the grief-stricken Achilles became a changed man. Donning a new suit of armor, he went to Agamemnon and patched up their feud. Then Achilles led the Greeks in a fierce charge against the Trojan ranks. Many of the gods, who backed one side or the other, joined in the fight. Zeus made thunder crash from the sky, and Poseidon made the earth quake and shook the hilltops.

Unable to withstand the Greek assault, the Trojans fled back inside the city. Only Hector remained outside the gates, waiting to face Achilles. Hector did not have to wait long. A few moments later, Achilles rushed at him. With a thunderous crash of bronze on bronze, the two heroes came together in a fight to the death. Cheers went up from the Greek and Trojan spectators, each side urging on its champion. Achilles was the first to hurl his spear, but he missed. Then Hector let loose his own spear. It hit his opponent's shield dead center but bounced off.

Cursing, Hector drew his sword and charged at Achilles. The Greek quickly recovered his spear and searched for an opening somewhere on Hector's

Having slain Hector, Achilles drags the body behind his chariot before Troy's walls.

body. Finally, Achilles saw that Hector's throat was momentarily exposed. There, Achilles drove his weapon. Brave Hector collapsed, and soon the fog of death descended on his eyes.

The Wooden Horse and Troy's End

Having defeated Hector, Achilles completed his vengeance. He stripped off Hector's armor and tied the corpse to the back of his chariot. Then Achilles dragged the body around the city walls. In time, though, Achilles' anger subsided. He agreed to give Hector's body to the grieving King Priam. The Trojans then conducted a solemn funeral for Hector; at the same time, the Greeks held final rites for Patroclus.

The war continued, however. And eventually, Achilles, like Hector, met his end in combat. Prince Paris, who was an expert bowman, killed Achilles with an arrow, which the god Apollo guided to its target. Then, in his turn, Paris met a similar fate when a Greek warrior shot him with a well-aimed arrow. The killing went on and on, and more men from both sides met their deaths.

Finally, the crafty Odysseus told the other Greek leaders that he had a plan that would end the war. At his urging, the Greeks constructed a large wooden horse. They left the horse and sailed away. Thinking the Greeks had given up the fight, the joyful Trojans flooded forth from their city and danced on the windswept plain. The Trojans thought the huge

A carving on a large vase shows Greek warriors climbing out of the wooden horse.

Helen, queen of Sparta. Her abduction by a Trojan led to war.

horse was an offering to the gods, so they dragged it into Troy.

This proved to be a grave mistake. What the Trojans did not know was that the horse was hollow. Odysseus and several other Greeks were hiding inside. That night, they crawled out of the horse's belly. They killed the guards and flung open the gates for the rest of the Greeks, who had sailed back under the cover of darkness. A great slaughter began. Cries of agony could be heard everywhere, and the bodies of the dead filled all the streets and houses.

On that terrible night, Priam's city fell to the triumphant Greeks. They killed the king and most of the other Trojan leaders. And the victors carried away the surviving Trojan women as slaves. Meanwhile, Menelaus reclaimed his wife, Helen. The woman whose beauty had caused the deaths of many brave heroes reluctantly turned her face toward Greece and home.

Chapter Four

Three Timeless Tales of Love

Greek mythology features numerous tales of love and lovers. Some end sadly, while others conclude on a note of hope or joy. Three of the most famous of these myths are the stories of Pyramis and Thisbe, Orpheus and Eurydice, and Alcestis and Admetus. The main ancient source of the story of Alcestis and Admetus is the play *Alcestis* by the ancient Greek playwright Euripides. The other two tales were told by the first-century B.C. Roman poet Ovid. His *Metamorphoses* is a large and important surviving source of ancient myths and legends. Ovid did not invent these love stories, of course. They had been part of Greek and Roman lore for many centuries. One, the tale of Pyramis and Thisbe, actually originated in the Middle East and eventually made its way to Greece.

Pyramis and Thisbe

In fact, Pyramis and Thisbe's sad story is set in the most famous city in the ancient Middle East: Babylon

The witty Roman poet Ovid composed a huge book of Greco-Roman myths.

(in what is now Iraq). Pyramis and Thisbe were two young people who lived next door to each other. Because their families' houses shared a common wall, they became well acquainted. And eventually they fell in love and wanted to get married. Unfortunately, their parents did not approve of the relationship and tried to keep them apart. This did not stop the lovers from communicating secretly, however. They found a crack in the wall between their homes, a small slit that no one had seen. Every day, the lovers talked to each other in whispers. They pressed their lips against the wall and moaned quietly about their sad situation.

Finally, Pyramis and Thisbe could stand their separation no longer. They planned to escape from their parents and run away together. They agreed to meet late one night near a tall mulberry tree covered with snow-white berries. Thisbe arrived first. Suddenly, she saw a lion approaching, its jaws covered with blood after a recent kill. Fearing that the beast might kill her too, she fled. But in her haste, she dropped her cloak. The curious beast sniffed it, then tore it to shreds before trotting away.

A Fatal Mistake

Only seconds later, Pyramis arrived. He found the blood-stained remnants of the cloak and assumed that Thisbe had been killed. The youth was overcome with grief. So he plunged a knife into his chest. And as he fell, his blood spurted out over the white mulberries, staining them red. Not long afterward,

Shakespeare's tale of star-crossed lovers, Romeo and Juliet, was partly based on the tale of Pyramis and Thisbe.

Thisbe returned. Seeing her lover lying on the ground and gasping his last breaths, she decided to die with him. Using the same knife he had, she ended her life.

When Pyramis's and Thisbe's parents discovered what had happened, they were filled with shame and sorrow. The hearts of the gods, who had watched from above, were also filled with pity. So they created a lasting tribute to the tragic lovers. The gods decided that from that day forward the mulberry would bear only deep red fruit.

Orpheus and Eurydice

Like Pyramis, Orpheus was a handsome young man. A Greek poet and musician, Orpheus was blessed with an amazing talent. When he sang and played his harp, all nearby people, animals, and even rocks and trees stood still, moved to tears by the beauty of his songs.

Orpheus eventually met and married Eurydice, a beautiful young woman. He loved her deeply and they lived happily together for a short time. But then a poisonous snake bit Eurydice and she died. Orpheus was devastated by this loss. He could not eat or sleep.

The young man decided to try to overcome death and get his wife back. He daringly descended into the Underworld. There, he confronted Hades and Persephone, the rulers of the realm of the dead. The man began playing his harp and singing a beautiful song. The words told how he had come to find Eurydice, an innocent and carefree girl. Orpheus begged the gods to allow her to return to the earth with him and share his love. If they refused, he said, he would give up his own life so that he could live with her in the Underworld.

Orpheus's words and tune were so sad and haunting that Hades, Persephone, and numerous listening ghosts began weeping. The mighty lord of darkness

This nineteenth-century painting shows the fateful moment when Orpheus looks back at Eurydice.

could not find it in his heart to refuse the man's plea. Hades called out to Eurydice and allowed her to leave with Orpheus and rejoin the living. The one condition was that Orpheus must walk ahead of his wife and not look back at her until they reached the earth's surface.

During most of the long trek out of the Underworld, Orpheus followed the god's orders and did not look back. But at the last moment, the man could no longer resist the temptation. He turned to gaze on Eurydice's lovely face. And he watched in horror as the startled young woman was sucked back into the depths, never to return.

After that, Orpheus tried to reenter Hades' dark kingdom, hoping to join his twice-dead wife. But the lord of the dead would not let him in. The unhappy Orpheus became a hermit, shunning the company of his fellow humans. But this did not make him feel any better. For the rest of his days, he had to live with the memory of his mistake. Later, others would learn a lesson from that mistake: Those who disobey the gods should expect to pay a terrible price.

Alcestis and Admetus

The tale of Alcestis and Admetus also involves an attempt to cheat death, but with a decidedly different outcome. The god Apollo helped Admetus, the king of Pherae (in northern Greece), win the hand of Alcestis, a princess of a neighboring city. The god also granted Admetus the privilege of escaping death. All the man had to do was find another mortal who would willingly take his place when it was his time to die.

When that time came, Alcestis offered to die in her husband's place. She lay down atop a stone altar in the palace and waited for Thanatos, god of death, to take her away to the Underworld. As the hours passed, the palace grew unnaturally quiet. Admetus and the couple's relatives, friends, and servants sat grief stricken and weeping.

At this fateful moment, the great hero Heracles happened by the palace on his way to perform one of his twelve labors. Hearing so many people sobbing at once, the strongman was perplexed. Then a servant told him the sad circumstances of Alcestis's death.

A bronze statue of Apollo, the god who granted Admetus a means of escaping death.

Moved by the story of the woman's love and loyalty, the big-hearted Heracles decided to stop Thanatos from taking Alcestis. The strongman hid and waited for the god to appear.

When Thanatos finally approached, Heracles leapt on him and locked his arms around the surprised god's chest. Then the man wrestled his opponent to the floor. Their muscular bodies thrashed around the room as they fought. Eventually, Heracles was victorious and the figure of death gave up and withdrew.

A few minutes later, Heracles approached Admetus, followed by a woman wearing a veil across her face. The king should accept this woman into his home, said the strongman. But Admetus refused. No woman, no matter how beautiful or wonderful, he said, could take the place of his beloved Alcestis. Then Heracles revealed that the woman was none other than Alcestis herself. Thanks to the courage of Greece's greatest hero, the two lovers were happily reunited.

The tales of Pyramis and Thisbe and Orpheus and Eurydice end sadly because of tragic mistakes. Thisbe left her bloodied cloak where Pyramis would find it and fear the worst. And Orpheus disobeyed the gods. By contrast, Alcestis's only mistake was loving her husband enough to die for him. The Greeks could not allow such a story to end sadly.

For Further Exploration

Isaac Asimov, *The Greeks: A Great Adventure*. Boston: Houghton Mifflin, 1965. An excellent, entertaining overview of Greek history and culture.

David Bellingham, *An Introduction to Greek Mythology*. Secaucus, NJ: Chartwell Books, 1989. Explains the major Greek myths and legends and their importance to the ancient Greeks. Contains many beautiful photos and drawings.

Peter Connolly, *The Legend of Odysseus*. New York: Oxford University Press, 1986. An excellent, easy-to-read summary of the events of Homer's *Iliad* and *Odyssey*, including many informative sidebars about the way people lived in early Greek times. Also contains many stunning illustrations re-creating the fortresses, homes, ships, and armor of the period.

Homer, *Iliad*. Retold by Barbara Leonie Picard. New York: Oxford University Press, 1960; Homer, *Odyssey*. Retold by Barbara Leonie Picard. New York: Oxford University Press, 1952. Easy-to-follow, quick-moving introductions to Homer's classic works, which shaped Greece's mythology and national character.

Charles Kingsley, *The Heroes*. Santa Rosa, CA: Classics

Press, 1968. Presents superb retellings of the famous ancient Greek myths of Jason and the Golden Fleece, Perseus and Medusa, Theseus and the Minotaur, and the labors of Heracles.

Don Nardo, *The Greenhaven Encyclopedia of Greek and Roman Mythology*. San Diego: Greenhaven Press, 2002. A huge collection of short articles about all of the important heroes, kings, gods, and places in ancient Greek and Roman myths. The reading level is junior high school.

Susan Peach and Anne Millard, *The Greeks*. London: Usborne, 1990. A general overview of the history, culture, myths, and everyday life of ancient Greece, presented in a format suitable to young, basic readers.

Index

Achilles, 25, 26, 28–30
Admetus, 34, 40–42
Agamemnon (king of Mycenae), 25, 26, 28
Age of Heroes, 15
Ajax, 25
Alcestis, 34, 40–42
Alcestis (Euripides), 34
Aphrodite (goddess of love), 9
Apollo (god of prophecy, truth, and healing), 9
   Admetus and, 40
   oracle of, 16, 22
   Trojan War and, 30
Ares (god of war), 9
Artemis (goddess of the moon), 9
Athena (goddess of wisdom and war), 9, 19
Augeas, stables of, 18

Babylon, 34
Briareos, 6

centaurs, 22
Cerberus, 19
Cerynitian Hind, 18
Chaos, 5
Classical Age, 14
Cottus, 6
creation
   of early gods, 5–7
   of humans, 10–11
   of Olympians, 8–10
Creon (king of Thebes), 16
Cronos, 7
curiosity, 11, 13
cyclopes, 7

Darkness. *See* Erebus
Delphi, oracle of, 16, 22
Demeter (goddess of agriculture), 8, 9
democracy, 14

earthquakes, 6
Erebus, 5
Eros (god of love), 5
Euripides, 34
Eurydice, 34, 38–40, 42
Eurystheus (king of Mycenae), 16

Father Sky. *See* Uranus
fire, 11

Gaia (Mother Earth), 6–8
Geryon, 18
giants, 20
gods and goddesses
   creation of early, 5–7
   creation of Olympian, 8–10
   described, 4
   disobeying of, 40
   Pyramis and Thisbe and, 37
   see also specific gods and goddesses
Gyes, 6

Hades (god of Underworld), 9
   birth of, 8
   Heracles and, 20
   Orpheus and, 38–39
Hector (Trojan prince)
   attack led by, 26–28
   death of, 28–30
   described, 26
Helen (queen of Sparta), 25, 33
Hephaestos (god of fire and forges), 10–11
Heracles
   Alcestis and, 41–42
   crime of, 16
   described, 15–16
   giants and, 20
   labors of, 16–20
   on Mt. Olympus, 20, 22–23
Hera (wife and sister of Zeus)
   birth of, 8
   Heracles and, 16
   realm of, 9

Hermes (messenger god), 9
  Heracles and, 19
  Pandora and, 11
Hestia (goddess of the hearth), 8, 9
Hippolyta (queen of the Amazons),
  18
Homer, 24
humans, 10–11
Hydra, 17–18

Iliad (Homer), 24

Love. *See* Eros

Megra, 16
Menelaus (king of Sparta), 25, 33
Metamorphoses (Ovid), 34
Mother Earth. *See* Gaia
Mt. Olympus, 9, 20, 22–23
mulberry, 38
Mycenae, 16

Nemean Lion, 17
Night. *See* Nyx
Nyx (child of Chaos), 5

Oceanus, 7
Odysseus, 25, 30
Olympians, 8–10
  see also specific gods and goddesses
Olympic Games, 14
Orpheus, 34, 38–40, 42
Ovid, 34

Pandora, 11, 13
Paris (Trojan prince), 25, 30
Patroclus, 26–28, 30
Persephone, 38–39
Poseidon (god of sea), 9
  birth of, 8

Trojan War and, 28
Priam (king of Troy), 26
Prometheus, 10–11
Pyramis, 34, 36–38, 42

rebellions
  of Cronos, 7
  of Zeus, 8–9
Rhea, 7

Tartarus, 6, 7, 9
Tethys, 7
Thanatos (god of death), 40, 41–42
theater, 14
Thisbe, 34, 36–38, 42
Titans, 7, 10–11
Trojan War
  beginning of, 25–26
  combat between Achilles and
    Hector during, 28–30
  gods and, 28, 30
  Greek attack and, 28
  Trojan attack and, 26–28
  Trojan horse and, 30, 32–33

Underworld
  Heracles and, 19
  Orpheus in, 38
  ruler of, 9
Uranus (Father Sky), 6–9

volcanoes, 6

Zeus
  birth of, 7
  children of, 9
  Heracles and, 16, 20
  Pandora and, 11, 13
  Prometheus and, 10, 11
  Trojan War and, 28

Picture Credits

About the Author

A historian and award-winning writer, Don Nardo has written or edited numerous books about ancient Greece and Rome for young people of all ages. Among these are *Life in Ancient Athens, Greek and Roman Sport, Life of a Roman Soldier, Games of Ancient Rome,* and *The Greenhaven Encyclopedia of Greek and Roman Mythology.* He lives with his wife, Christine, in Massachusetts.